Booklover's Book of
Jokes, Quips & Quotes

In memory of Jonathan Cornell (1971–2011),
who could always make me laugh

Booklover's
BOOK *of*
JOKES
Quips &
QUOTES

Compiled by David Wilkerson

THE BRITISH LIBRARY

First published 2011 by
The British Library
96 Euston Road
London NW1 2DB

Collection copyright © 2011 The British Library
Compiled by David Wilkerson

British Library Cataloguing-in-Publication Data
A Catalogue record for this book is available from
The British Library

ISBN 978 0 7123 5842 2

Text designed and typeset by illuminati, Grosmont
Cover design by Andrew Barron @ thextension

Printed and bound in Hong Kong
by Great Wall Printing Co. Ltd

CONTRIBUTORS

Kate Bates	Catherine Britton
Katherine Clark	Beth Cleall
Jonathan Cornell	Daphne Day
Susan Green	Jenny Lawson
Martin Oestreicher	Ann Parker
Ben Richardson	Ellie Russell
Lara Speicher	David Way
Margaret Webb	Mark Whitley
Alison Wilkerson	Amy Wilkerson
Brian Wilkerson	Chris Wilkerson
David Wilkerson	Hannah Yates

Jokes from *Yorkshire Humour* reproduced with kind permission
of Mark Whitley of Country Publications Ltd.

Whilst every endeavour has been made to correctly attribute work
and seek permission to reference, we will of course correct any
errors or omissions in future editions. Any errors are my
responsibility alone, for which I apologise profusely
and congratulate you on your keen eye.
David Wilkerson

Contents

'It's all very well to be able to write books,
but can you waggle your ears?'

J.M. Barrie to H.G. Wells

Some literary jokes

What does the skeleton get up to when she pops into her local library?

She likes to bone up on her favourite topic.

What does the mummy do when he goes to his local library?

He gets himself all wrapped up in a good book.

Why does the ghost keep coming back to the library for more books?

Because she goes through them far too quickly.

What do young ghost-hunters do their homework in?

Exorcise books.

Why should you be careful when reading a book by a ghostwriter?

It's got no spine.

Why don't elephants ever pay overdue fines?

They always bring their books back on time.
An elephant never forgets!

Why does an elephant use his trunk as a bookmark?

So that he always nose his place.

Why didn't the skeleton come back to the library with an overdue book?

He was too gutless and spineless.

What has a spine but no bones?

A book, of course.

Which mythical king of England used a round table to write lots of books?

King Author!

If you were lost in the woods, who would you trust for directions: the publisher who prints everything you write, the White Queen, the Good Fairy, Santa Claus or an agent?

The agent. The others don't exist and you are hallucinating.

What did the detective do when he didn't believe the librarian's tale?

He booked her!

Where does a librarian sleep?

Between the covers.

What do librarians have their meals on?

A bookplate.

Literary light bulb jokes

How many aspiring writers does it take to change a light bulb?

1,001... one to change the light bulb and the other thousand to say 'I could have done that!'

How many librarians does it take to change a light bulb?

No idea, but I know where you can look it up!

How many library technicians does it take to change a light bulb?

Eleven. One to follow approved process, and ten to review the procedure and recommend future policy changes.

How many science fiction writers does it take to change a light bulb?

Two, but it's actually the same person doing it. He went back in time and met himself in the doorway and then the first one sat on the second one's shoulders so that he was able to reach it. Then a major time-slip paradox occurred, and the entire room and all the contents slipped through a time portal into a parallel universe.

How many library managers does it take to change a light bulb?

Well, first we need to form a committee to determine who exactly will be affected by the change, then we need to ensure all appropriate staff have attended the Managing Change training course, then we need to form a Light Bulb Strategy Focus Group to ensure that the change is made using the best-practice guidelines, appointing a Project Manager to lead the Change Transition process and ensuring that counselling is available for those affected by the disruption and that the budgetary effect has been taken into account...
Oh, you've changed it.

How many crime writers does it take to change a light bulb?

Two. One to screw it almost all the way in, and the other to give it a surprising and unexpected twist at the end.

☞ **Conversations in the local library**

Borrower: You are lucky to get this book back:
     my dog was eating it.
Librarian: How did you manage to rescue it?
Borrower: Oh, I just took the words right out of his
     mouth.

Borrower: Excuse me, where's the self-help section?
Librarian: Look for yourself.

Borrower: Excuse me, sorry to interrupt, I wonder if
     you could possibly help me and tell me where are
     the books on assisting people with low self-
     esteem? If you don't mind. Sorry, I realize that
     you are busy. Sorry.
Librarian: Why don't you stop wasting everyone's
     time, you pathetic specimen and just get lost and
     rot away somewhere.

Borrower: Excuse me where's the section on
     pantomime?
Librarian: It's behind you!
Borrower: Oh no, it's not!
Librarian: Oh yes, it is!

Borrower: Excuse me, can you tell me where the books on suicide are?

Librarian: No, you lot never bring the books back.

Borrower: Excuse me, where are the books on archaeology?

Librarian: They'll take some digging out.

Borrower: Excuse me, do you have any guides to using sarcasm?

Librarian: Of course we do sir, thousands and thousands, it's a really popular area, in fact we rarely stock anything else as it's all people want.

Borrower: Do you have any books on positive thinking?

Librarian: We certainly do, we have loads and loads, yes, yes, yes. You've certainly come to the right place. Boy, do we have some books for you. There's nothing we like more than to be able to offer you a vast selection. We aspire to help – you are our life, our joy, our reason for being.

Borrower: Excuse me, do you have any books on the use of rhetoric?

Librarian: I'm sorry sir, I'm afraid that I don't answer rhetorical questions.

Borrower: Excuse me, do you have any guides to casting spells?
Librarian: We used to, but we became disenchanted.

Borrower: Excuse me, do you have any books on great angling thefts?
Librarian: No, we tried them once but no one took the bait.

☞ In the local bookshop

I went into my local bookshop and asked if they stocked any books on pessimism...
   but they said that there was no point because no one would ever buy them.

I went into my local bookshop and asked if they stocked any books on speculative investments...
   but they said it was too risky.

I went into my local bookshop and asked if they stocked any books on forbearance...
   but they wouldn't tolerate the idea.

I went into my local bookshop and asked if they stocked any books on camping holidays...
   their reaction was intense.

I went into my local bookshop and asked if they stocked any books on campanology...
  but they said that it didn't ring any bells.

I went into my local bookshop and asked if they stocked any books on paranoia...
  they just wanted to know who was asking and why.

I went into my local bookshop and asked if they stocked any books on meddling...
  but they told me to mind my own business.

I went into my local bookshop and asked if they stocked any books on apathy...
  but they said that there was no interest, no one ever bought the books and what was the point anyway.

I went into my local bookshop and asked if they stocked any books on contemplation...
  they said that they would think about it.

I went into my local bookshop and asked if they stocked any books on fortune-telling...
  but they said that there was no prophet in it.

Sherlock Holmes and Watson are on the trail of a suspect. 'Look Holmes, an impression of a foot,' says Watson suddenly. 'No time for your silly impressions now, Watson,' Holmes replies.

Shakespeare walks into a pub one day and the bartender says: 'Oi! You can't come in here.' Shakespeare asks why not and the bartender answers: 'I keep telling you, you're bard!'

An Irish guy goes for a job on a building site. The foreman interviewing him asks him if he knows the difference between a girder and a joist.

The Irish guy replies, 'Goethe wrote *Faust*; Joyce wrote *Ulysses*.'

The English-language tutor was lecturing to his writing skills class of aspiring writers. 'In English,' he said, 'a double negative forms a positive. In some languages, though, such as Russian, a double negative is still a negative. However, there is no language wherein a double positive can form a negative.'

A young prospective novelist from the back of the class responded, 'Yeah, right.'

One day, during his weekly visit to the local library, a mature gentleman decides to throw caution to the wind and makes a tentative approach to a young female librarian. He walks up to the counter and says, 'I have heard it said often that when a man reaches a certain distinguished age he becomes rather attractive to younger ladies. Have you heard that at all?'

'Oh yes,' she replies brightly. 'It's something I am asked a lot, sir. Try the shelves to my right, Romantic Fiction & Fantasy. Oh, and failing that, it might be worth checking in Popular Psychology, there's a small selection of titles on Delusional Thinking!'

Due to the government cutbacks, many public libraries have been supplementing their revenue by setting up coffee shops and restaurants within their buildings. One major library has announced record profits after employing celebrity chefs to cook for their users. The library concerned is refusing to name the celebrities, as they believe that other libraries will copy its idea and its chefs will be tempted away to work elsewhere.

The government has authorized an investigation to discover who is responsible for this initiative. In other words, they really want to know who exactly has been booking the cooks!

Coming to the end of his first job interview at a major publisher, the Human Resources manager asked the arrogant young aspiring editor, fresh out of university, 'What sort of starting salary were you looking for?'

The applicant says rather smugly, 'For starters I'd look for around the £75,000 mark, depending on the benefits package and how you match up to other offers I am considering.'

The interviewer said, 'Well, what would you say to a package of 35 days annual paid leave, full private medical cover, a pension entitlement to match the best in the business, free membership of a nearby exclusive gym, a company credit card with a £5,000 a month personal expenses facility, no questions asked, and a company car of your choice to a value of £50,000, all running costs paid for, of course.'

The young lad tried to control his excitement, but sat straight up and said, 'Wow, absolutely fantastic! Are you kidding?'

'Course I am,' said the interviewer, 'But you started it!'

Ex-President George Bush finally makes his first visit to a library; he ask the librarian if he can take out a book on the war against Iraq.

'Don't be silly,' says the librarian. 'You know you'll never finish it.'

A publisher was captured by cannibals whilst on a trekking holiday. He is trussed up and put into a cooking pot of boiling water.

'What do you do?' politely enquires the salivating cannibal Chief.

'I am an editor,' the publisher replies.

'Well,' says the cannibal, 'congratulations, in a way you are about to be promoted. Very soon you'll be an editor-in-chief!'

Life seems full of woe for John, nothing seems to work, things always finish badly, relationships always fail, he can't hold down a job, everyone seems to let him down. So, determined to keep a positive outlook, he pops into his local bookshop and buys an audio CD set called *How to Handle Life's Disappointments*.

He rushes home and eagerly opens the case. It is empty.

I have just heard on the news that the valuable collection of rare novels stolen recently has been found safe, and surprisingly arranged in a perfect alphabetical sequence.

The police suspect Organised Crime.

A shy schoolgirl was very excited about the book she found in the library called *How* to *Hug*.

Unfortunately it was volume 7 of a dictionary.

An aspiring author arrives home to see the wreck of his burned-down house. His hysterical wife is standing outside. 'What the hell happened?' asks the man.

'Oh, John, it was awful, I was cooking and the phone rang. It was your agent,' she splutters. 'Because I was on the phone, I didn't notice the oil in the frying pan had caught fire. Suddenly there was a great whoosh and the whole area was covered in flames. I barely made it out alive. Everything is gone. Our darling cat Felix didn't make it, the canaries are dead, I've lost all the mementos from my mother, your dad's war medals, the children's Christmas presents...'

'Wait, wait. Hold on a minute,' the man says. 'Did you say that my agent called?'

A famous but grouchy author was asked to contribute a short story for a book in support of a worthy charity. The themes he was given to work on were Religion, Sex and Mystery.

Under great pressure to comply and be seen to be supportive, the miserable old git submitted: 'Good God, she's pregnant, I wonder who did it?'

Odd titles

All booksellers and librarians have their favourite
'Asked fors'. Here is just a flavour.

The Odd Sea (Homer, *The Odyssey*)

Oranges and Peaches (Charles Darwin, *The Origin of Species*)

How to Kill a Mocking Bird (Harper Lee, *To Kill a Mockingbird*)

Lord of the Files (William Golding, *Lord of the Flies*)

Bonfire of the Vampires (Tom Wolfe, *Bonfire of the Vanities*)

100 Years of Playing Solitaire (Gabriel García Márquez, *One Hundred Years of Solitude*)

A book on bog art (A book on actor Humphrey Bogart)

Midnight Cowboy (Salman Rushdie, *Midnight's Children*)

The Brothers Carry Them Off (Fyodor Dostoevsky, *The Brothers Karamazov*)

Honour Road (Jack Kerouac, *On the Road*)

Dr Wells Fargo (Boris Pasternak, *Doctor Zhivago*)

The Adventures of Huckleberry Hound (Mark Twain, *The Adventures of Huckleberry Finn*)

The Great Gas Bill (F. Scott Fitzgerald, *The Great Gatsby*)

Donkey Oats (Miguel de Cervantes, *Don Quixote*)

Christopher Shandy (Laurence Sterne, *Tristram Shandy*)

Anna, Karen and Ena (Leo Tolstoy, *Anna Karenina*)

Yet more literary jokes

What is Shakespeare's favourite meal?
Scrambled eggs and Hamlet.

What's a phantom's favourite book called?
Ghouliver's Travels.

What's a witch's favourite book called?
Broom at the Top.

What is green and purple, hangs out in gangs and wants revenge?
The Grapes of Wrath.

Did you hear about the leper who went into a bookshop and said 'Have you got *My Left Foot*?'

What is Harper Lee's favourite drink?
Tequila Mockingbird.

What did they call Tom Sawyer's friend after he lost a lot of weight?
Huckleberry Thin.

What would you get if you crossed a locomotive with the author of *Tom Sawyer*?
A choo choo Twain.

How did the author of *Tom Sawyer* learn to ride a bicycle?
With Twaining wheels.

What book is about a rodent pioneer in America?
Little Mouse on the Prairie.

What do you get if you cross a werewolf with a sculptor?
Hairy Potter.

Those Harry Potter books are so unrealistic. Honestly, a ginger-haired kid with two friends!

Librarian: Did you enjoy reading *Moby Dick*?
Reader: I couldn't finish it. I got seasick.

Why do airline pilots refuse to stop near Peter Pan's house?
Because of the sign saying 'Never Never Land'.

Why did the vampire buy books on drawing?
He wanted to know how to draw blood.

Did you hear about the German vampire who became a poet?
He went from bad to verse.

What happened when the bloodhound wrote his autobiography?
It got on the best-smeller list.

Did you read the dachshund's autobiography?
It's a long story.

I bought a book on repetition the other day.
Same old story.

If anyone is thinking about buying an autobiography, I don't want to ruin the ending for you, but it's only fair that you know that in the end they always write a book.

The librarian told me that books are man's best friend, so my dog bit him.

Why was the library so messy?
Because it was full of litter-ature.

Why did the rabbit go to the library?
He wanted to burrow a book.

Why won't you find any books in Prague's public library?
They're all Czeched out.

What books do the banks order from Prague?
Czech books.

Why did the Romanian stop reading for the night?
To give his Bucharest.

When the cold wind blows, what does a book do?
It puts on a book jacket.

What's the difference between a boring book and a boring guest?
You can shut the book up.

If a borrower goes to a seven-storey library and takes out seven novels, how many are left?
None. The library had only seven stories.

What did the spider do inside the library computer?
It made a web page.

Did Shakespeare stare at the Queen?
No, it was more of a Lear.

Where are there more nobles than in the royal court?

In the library, where all the books have titles.

When a knight reads a book, who will always be at his side?

His page.

What's the difference between comedy and drama in Russian plays?

In both, everyone dies, but in the comedies they die happy.

What's the difference between a fisherman and a reluctant schoolboy?

One baits his hooks and the other hates his books.

Where does success come before work and after idleness?

In the dictionary.

Why did the bird fly into the bookshop?

It was looking for bookworms.

If you don't know what the word 'dictionary' means, where would you look it up?

My father gave me a really cheap dictionary for my birthday.

But I just couldn't find the words to thank him.

I wrote a book about a transsexual with a speech impediment.

It's called *Man or Myth*.

I asked my local library for a book on the warfare of the ninth century and was told that all the books had been withdrawn as they contained far too much Saxon violence.

I went into a bookshop to get a book on camouflage the other day.

I couldn't find one anywhere.

Bookseller: Do you like Kipling?
Customer: I'm not sure if I've ever done it!

Librarian: Knock, knock.
Borrower: Who's there?
Librarian: Winnie.
Borrower: Winnie who?
Librarian: Winnie you going to return that
    Dan Brown book?

Librarian: Knock knock.

Borrower: Who's there?

Librarian: Winnie Thup.

Borrower: Winnie Thup who?

Librarian: He's in the Young Fiction section with Piglet and Eeyore!

Librarian: Knock knock.

Borrower: Who's there?

Librarian: Clothes on.

Borrower: Clothes on who?

Librarian: The Library's clothes on Christmas Day, but we'll be open again on Thursday!

Looking for a well-known story for her granddaughter, an elderly customer asks the bookseller if they have a copy of *Bambi*. 'Yes,' says the bookseller, 'but I am afraid that it's a little dear.'

We had a surgeon in our shop the other day. He was browsing through a book but when he got to the end he got very concerned.

Apparently he didn't like the look of the appendix.

A frog walks into his local bookshop and asks the bookseller what good novels he'd recommend.

But every time he comes up with suggestions the frog dismisses them 'Reddit, reddit, reddit'.

A customer walks into a bookshop. 'Do you sell stationery?' he enquires.

'Not always,' says the bookseller, 'sometimes I skip about a bit as I ring things up.'

Two retired academics are sitting passing the time on the balcony at their gentlemen's club.

One, a History scholar, asks the other, a Professor of Philosophy, 'I presume that you have read Marx?'

To which the professor replies, 'Oh, indeed I have, it's these damn wicker chairs!'

Isn't it ironic that the best book-keepers are the people who borrow them and don't return them?

My teacher said that we should treat our schoolbooks just like we treat one another.

So after school I kicked the living daylights out of my History textbook.

Before Shakespeare became a writer he tried to be a sketch artist but had a hard time making up his mind which pencil to use.

It was always the same problem... 2B or not 2B?

I received a book on Feng Shui for my birthday.

I've absolutely no idea where to put it.

At Ted's retirement party, it falls upon his boss to say a few words and make the gift presentation.

'Great to see you all here tonight to say goodbye and thank you to our loyal colleague, Ted. Our Ted, who doesn't know the meaning of the words "impossible task", who never took the phrase "lunch hour" literally, who has refused to acknowledge the pressures of "timely presentation of work" and who couldn't understand the meaning of the words "strategically important". So, dear Ted, we have clubbed together to buy you... a dictionary!'

I have written a book myself actually. It will be published in time for Christmas and will be called *How to Get Along with Absolute Everybody*. Didn't actually write it all myself, some other stupid morons helped.

During the Spanish Civil War, a bird returns to her nest to find an unwanted squatter – a larger bird who is perching in the nest whilst writing a novel. An argument ensues as the interloper refuses to give up the nest. Two bird chums are flying past and hear the commotion. 'What's going on there?' says one . 'Oh,' his winged companion replied, 'It's her nest, him in way.'

An aspiring novelist died and was given the choice of going to heaven or hell. He decided to check out each place first. As the author descended into the fiery pits of hell, he saw row upon row of writers chained to their desks in a steaming hot warehouse. As they worked, they were repeatedly beaten and screamed at by horned demons.

'Oh my God,' said the novelist, rather inappropriately. 'Please let me see heaven now.'

A few moments later, as the author rose majestically into heaven, he saw rows of writers, chained to their desks in a steaming hot warehouse. As they worked, they were repeatedly beaten and screamed at by the most evil looking angels.

'Wait a minute,' said the writer. 'This is just as bad as hell!'

'Oh no, it's not,' an unseen voice responded. 'Here, your work actually gets published.'

Yorkshire humour

A note found in a library book: 'Joe, when you've read up to here, please take the pie out of the oven.'

A small girl from the country visited some friends in town. She gazed long and earnestly at their well-filled bookshelves, and then declared:

'We get books from the library van, too. But we have to return ours.'

In the village school they were having a lesson on books and libraries in preparation for the appearance of the library van.

'Does anyone know what the person in charge of the library is called?' asked the teacher.

'Yes, miss,' said a small boy. 'A bookie.'

The parson called upon a farmer and found him reading the Bible. Three or four puppies were running round his feet.

'Well, this is a pleasure – to see you improving in your old age,' remarked the vicar.

Said the farmer, 'to tell you the truth, I'm looking for some names for the dogs.'

The parable of punctuation

Dear Jenny,

I so want a woman who really knows what love is all about. You are genuine, kind, thoughtful and gracious. People who are not the same as you admit to being horrible and nasty, without any redeeming features.

You have ruined me for other women. I yearn for you. I have no feelings whatsoever when we are apart. I could be happy forever – please will you let me be yours?

Desmond.

or

Dear Jenny,

I so want a woman who really knows what love is. All about you are genuine, kind, thoughtful and gracious people, who are not the same as you. Admit to being horrible and nasty, without any redeeming features.

You have ruined me. For other women I yearn. For you I have no feelings whatsoever. When we are apart I could be happy forever. Please will you let me be?

Yours,

Desmond.

Book titles (maybe)

Talking Straight, Frank Lee Speaking
The Start of the Year, Jan Ury
Clear a Room, Bea Bore
Droopy Drawers, Lucy Lastic
Fighting Wild Cats, Claude Face
Selling Flowers, Flo Wrist
Time to Skate, I.C. Rivers
Giving Evidence, Tess T. Fie
A Life in Sprinting, Hebe Quick
Watch Yourself, Bea Hayve
The Story of a Lighthouse, Eddie Stone
Why It Doesn't Work, Mal Funshun
Keep Intruders Out, Barb Dwyer
I Sat on the Cat, Claude Bottom
Take a Day Off, Colin Seeck
Split Personality, Jacqueline Hyde
Big Brother, Will B. Watchinu
Davy Crockett's Famous Battle, Al A. Moe
Smashing Glass, Ivor Stone
The Leaking Tap, Constant Dripping
Profit from Wills, Benny Fishery
The History of Sprinting, C.M. Run
A Breakfast Treat, Hammond Eggs
Jake the Pake, Peg Legg

A View on Apathy, Hugh Kares
The Pasta Cook, Al Dentay
An Unhappy Mind, Maud Lynn Forts
Travelling in China, Rick Sure
Modern Haircuts, Sean Head
Crossing the Desert, I. Rhoda Kamel
Shhhh! Don't Wake the Baby, Elsie Crys
Making Peace, Olive Branch
My Visit to the Dentist, R. Euan Payne
Keep Fit, Work Out, Jim Nasium
Conundrums, N. Igmas
A Day at the Races, Wilma Moneylast
Working for Charity, Ben Nevolent
Teach Yourself Good Oarsmanship, Roman Roe
My Life in Scrap, Orson Kartt
Spud Tyrant, Dick Tater
Walking to Work Again, Miss Dee Bus
Lots of Fuss, Hugh N. Kry
It Just Happened, Oliver Suddan
Winning, Vic Tree
Having an Operation, Neil Bimouth
Disgusting Foods, Henrietta Slug
Archery for Beginners, Beau N. Arrow
I Need to Leave the Room, Isadore Open
The Last Month of the Year, Dee Sember
Happy To Be Finished, Gladys Allover
Visit Europe, Frances Closest

Give Us Your Money, Andy Tover
Tights for the Gym, Leo Tarred
An Acceptable Round of Golf, Paris Goode
Wish You Luck, Bess Twishes
The Peeping Tom, Sawyer Drawers
The Mother-in-Law Arrives, Greta Nicely
No Standing Room, Sid Downe
An Outdoors Life, Al Freskoe
Getting into Debt, Owen Kash
Stylish Gym Wear, C.R. Shortz
No Qualifications, Manuel Labourer
Another Year Older, Abbie Burphday
Clean Clothes, Preston Ironed
No, Kurt Reply
Turning the Tables on Leo Tolstoy, Warren Peace
Ambitions and Dreams, Jason Rainbows
Not with Us, Ena Trance
Opening a Venetian Blind, Paul Down
Fighting Bulls, Matt A. Door
Meeting the Queen, Kurt C. Propelly
My Eating Disorder, Anna Wrecksier
Fighting Tiredness, I.M. Beat
Can It Be True?, Shirley U. Gest
March Into Battle, Sally Forth
Why It Happened, Murphy Sloor
The Perfect Dessert, Sue Phlay
Nothing To Do, I.M. Board

The Weather to Come, Wayne Fourkast
Snappy Times, Ali Gaytor
Chopping Trees, Tim Burr
The Naked Lady, Oliver Klozeroff
Bell-ringing for Beginners, Paul de Wrope
How to Pray, Neal Downe
Behave Like a Royal, Grave Foolie
Dumbo and His Chums, Ellie Funts
The Best Laser Weapon, Ray Gunn
Construction Made Simple, Jerry Build
Let's Include Everyone, Allan Sundry
Making Money from Libel, Sue Emall
What Is a Vacuum? M.T. Space
Studying the World Above Us, C.D. Skye
Robin Hood and Sherwood Forest, Robin D. Rich
The Garlic Eater, I Malone
How to Respond, Colin Bach
It Wasn't Me, Guv, Ivan Alibi
The Party Starts When the Sun Goes Down, Gladys
   Knight
Jack Be Nimble, Jack B. Quick
My Lovely Day at the Seaside, Sandy Beach
Get Caught by the Police, Kermit A. Krime
An Alternative to Cotton, Polly Ester
Learn to Play a Wind Instrument, Clara Nett
My Life in their Hands, Jay Walker
My Love of Paris, Frances Wunderfull

Choose Your Paint Carefully, Mat Orgloss
Back Me to Win, Betty Wont
The Prodigal Returns, Greta Son
My Secret Life as a Slimy Snail, Michelle Shame
How to Help People, Lynda Hand
My Terrible Life, Anne Guish
Selecting the Best Garden Water Feature, Lily Pond
How to Cross Roads Safely, Luke Bothways
Football's Worst Strikers, Mr Goal
A Princess in Art, Andrew Pictures
Keep it Simple, Ella Mann Tree
Heaven is Fun, Ellie Snot
How to Eat Trees, Norman Nor
Perfect Baking, Pat A. Cake
The Creaking Hinge, Russ T. Gates
Desperate for a Lavatory, Lewis Nereby
Early Tape Recording Storage, Cass Ett
The Crimeless State, Laura Norda
Don't Leave Without Me, Isa Coming
Fruit-Picking, Phil D. Basket
Allotment Gardening, Rosa Cabbages
She's a Lady, Ellie Snowman
Kidnapping for Beginners, Caesar Andhide
How to Find Something, Luke A. Round
Basic Addition, Adam Up
Looking after Sheep, Shep Hurd
A Valentine's Day Wish, Bea Mine

Bell Ringing for Beginners, Paul D. Rope
Sending Out Party Invitations, Maud D. Merrier
My Shameful Hobby, Robin Graves
Arithmetic Made Easy, Cal Q. Later
Take Your Hat Off, Seymour Hair
Struggling to Succeed, Willy Makeit
Divided by Borders, Miles Apart
My Life with Igor, Frank N. Stein
The Frozen River, I.C. Waters
Perfect Flooring, Walter Wall
Talking Rubbish, Stefan Nonsense
The Joys of Drinking, Al Coholic
Getting the Bargains, I.Q. Urly
How to Fall off a Cliff, Eileen Dover
You Can Do No Less, Minnie Mumm
The Changing World of Nappies, Dee Sposable
Bible Study, R.E. Classes
The Jewish Holiday, Hannah Kerr
Extreme Sports, Cliff Divers
Protective Headgear, Ivor Helmut
Use a Telescope, Seymour Starrs
Watching the Neighbours, Annette Curtain
Fighting Crocodiles, Claude Miarmoff
Be Fair, Sharon Sharalike
My Three Best Friends, Jill MacAnally
Don't Fade Away, Peter Out
Antibiotic Drugs, Penny Cillum

A Bit of a Leathering, Tanya Hyde
All about Lewis Carroll, Alison Wunderland
Where to Look Up Words, A. Dick Shunnery
A Hole in the Roof, Lee King
The Common Cold, I. Coffalot
Whodunnit, Howard E. Know
Flakey Shoulders, Dan Druff
Seasons Greetings, Mary Christmas
My Favourite Indoor Plant, Polly Anthus
Blow the Doors Off, Dina Mite
Got Away, Scot Free
A Very Poor Shot, Mrs Completely
Buy a House Made Simple, Bill Jerome Home
Bad Breath, Hal E. Tosis
Hair Hygiene, Dan Druff
Fun on the Beach, Rhoda Donkey
How to Make Money, Robin Banks
Winning the Lottery, Jack Pott
Squeeze a Spot, Lance A. Boyle
Robots and the Future, Cy Borg & Anne Droid
Why the Horse Bolted, Gay Topen
Hit Over the Head, Esau Starrs
Under Arrest, Hans Upp

Famous last words

Or purported to be. Why let truth and accuracy get in the way of an apt thought?

'I want nothing but death.' *Jane Austen*

'Now comes the mystery!' *Henry Ward Beecher*

'Bless you Sister. May all your sons be bishops.'
  Brendan Behan

'Take courage, Charlotte, take courage.' *Anne Brontë*

'Oh, I am not going to die, am I?' *Charlotte Brontë*

'If you will send for a doctor, I will see him now.'
  Emily Brontë

'Goodnight my darlings, I'll see you tomorrow.'
  Noël Coward

'I don't know which is more difficult in a Christian life, to live well or to die well.' *Daniel Defoe*

'I were miserable if I might not die. Thy kingdom come, thy will be done.' *John Donne*

'On the contrary!' *Henrik Ibsen* (in response to his wife remarking on an improvement in his health)

'Lift me up for I am dying. I shall die easy. Don't be frightened. Thank God it has come.' *John Keats*

'Maria, don't let me die.' *D.H. Lawrence*

'Mind your own business!' *Wyndham Lewis*

'Go on, get out! Last words are for fools who have not said enough!' *Karl Marx*

'God damn it, I knew it! Born in a hotel room and dying in a hotel room.' *Eugene O'Neill*

'Sister, you're trying to keep me alive as an old curiosity. But I'm done, I'm finished, I am going to die.' *George Bernard Shaw*

'I've just had eighteen whiskeys in a row. I do believe that is a record.' *Dylan Thomas*

'I am in a duel to death with this wallpaper. One or other of us has to go.' *Oscar Wilde*

BOOKS

Or else I sat on in my chamber green,
And liv'd my life, and thought my thoughts, and
     pray'd
My prayers without the vicar; read my books,
Without considering whether they were fit
To do me good. Mark, there. We get no good
By being ungenerous, even to a book,
And calculating profits... so much help
By so much rending. It is rather when
We gloriously forget ourselves, and plunge
Soul-forward, headlong, into a book's profound,
Impassion'd for its beauty and salt of truth–
'Tis then we get the right good from a book.

THE POETS

I had found the secret of a garret-room
Pil'd high with cases in my father's name;
Pil'd high, pack'd large, – where, creeping in and
     out
Among the giant fossils of my past,
Like some small nimble mouse between the ribs
Of a mastodon, I nibbled here and there
At this or that box, pulling through the gap,

In heats of terror, haste, victorious joy,
The first book first. And how I felt it beat
Under my pillow, in the morning's dark,
An hour before the sun would let me read!
My books!

Elizabeth Barrett Browning, *Aurora Leigh*

He ate and drank the precious Words,
His Spirit grew robust;
He knew no more that he was poor,
Nor that his frame was Dust.
He danced along the dingy Days,
And this Bequest of Wings
Was but a Book. What Liberty
A loosened spirit brings!

Emily Dickinson, *1587*

That book in many's eyes doth share the glory,
That in gold clasps locks in the golden story;
So shall you share all that he doth possess,
By having him, making yourself no less.

William Shakespeare, *Romeo and Juliet*

So, of his gentleness,
Knowing I loved my books, he furnish'd me
From mine own library with volumes that
I prize above my dukedom.

William Shakespeare, *The Tempest*

books, we know,
Are a substantial world, both pure and good:
Round these, with tendrils strong as flesh and blood,
Our pastime and our happiness will grow.

William Wordsworth, *Personal Talk*

Shakespearean barbs

'You would answer very well to a whipping.'

'scurvy, old, filthy, scurvy Lord!'

'France is a dog-hole.'

'She is too mean to have her name repeated.'

All's Well That Ends Well

'The most infectious pestilence upon thee!'

Anthony and Cleopatra

'like the toad, ugly and venomous.'

'Sweep on, you fat and greasy citizens!'

'Let's meet as little as we can.'

As You Like It

'I find the ass in compound with the major part of your syllables.'

'More of your conversation would infect my brain.'

'You are the musty chaff, and you are smelt above the moon.'

Coriolanus

'a thing too bad for bad report.'

'I have seen small reflection of her wit.'

'his celestial breath was sulphurous to smell.'

Cymbeline

'Frailty, thy name is woman.'

'It out-Herods Herod.'

'If thou dost marry, I'll give thee this plague for thy dowry.'

'Your bedded hair, like life in excrements, starts up and stand an end.'

'vicious mole of nature'

Hamlet

'I would have him poison'd with a pot of ale!'

'I am whipp'd and scourg'd with rods. Nettled, and stung with pismires, when I hear of this vile politician.'

'Peace, ye fat-guts!'

'Were't not for laughing I should pity him.'

'What a lack-brain is this!'

'Wilt thou rob this leathern-jerkin, crystal-button, knot-pated, agate-ring, puke-stocking, caddis-garter, smooth-tongue, Spanish pouch?'

Henry IV, Part 1

'He may keep his own grace, but he's almost out of mine, I can assure him.'

'You are as a candle, the better part burnt out.'

'Away, you scullion! You rampallian! You fustilarian! I'll tickle your catastrophe.'

'You whoreson upright rabbit!'

'Away, you cut-purse rascal, you filthy bung, away!'

'Away, you bottle-ale rascal, you basket-hilt stale juggler, you!'

'Is thy name Mouldy?

'Thou art a very ragged Wart.'

Henry IV, Part 2

'Thou cruel, ingrateful, savage and inhuman creature!'

'I should be angry with you if the time were convenient.'

'Here he comes, swelling like a turkey-cock.'

Henry V, Part 1

'You'll surely sup in hell.'

Henry VI, Part 2

'Thou misshapen Dick'

Henry VI, Part 3

'Wife of small wit.'

Henry VIII

'Out, dunghill!'

King John

'Thou whoreson zed! Thou unnecessary letter!'

'Thou art a boil, a plague-sore, or embossed carbuncle, in my corrupted blood.'

King Lear

'How now, you secret, black, and midnight hags!'

'Go, prick thy face, and over-red thy fear, thou lily-liver'd boy.'

Macbeth

'Your bum is the greatest about you; so that, in the beastliest sense, you are Pompey the Great.'

'He would mouth with a beggar though she smelt brown bread and garlic.'

Measure for Measure

'Froth and scum, thou liest!'

'Let vultures gripe thy guts!'

'I will knog his urinals about his knave's costard.'

The Merry Wives of Windsor

'You juggler! You canker-blossom!'

A Midsummer Night's Dream

'Here's a dish I love not! I cannot endure my Lady Tongue.'

Much Ado About Nothing

'May his pernicious soul rot half a grain a day!'

Othello

'Thou art the rudeliest welcome to this world.'

Pericles

'Blush, blush, thou lump of foul deformity'

'Out of my sight! Thou dost infect my eyes.'

Richard III

'I will bite thee by the ear for that jest.'

'Beautiful tyrant! fiend angelical!
Dove-feather'd raven! wolvish-ravening lamb!'

'Thou detestable maw, thou womb of death.'

Romeo and Juliet

'How foul and loathsome is thine image!'

'Lead apes in hell!'

'Away, you three-inch fool!'

'You peasant swain! You whoreson malt-horse drudge!'

The Taming of the Shrew

'Toads, beetles, bats, light on you!'

'Poor worm, thou art infected!'

The Tempest

'Thou disease of a friend!'

'Thy lips rot off!'

Timon of Athens

'I will beat thee into handsomeness!'

'Thou thing of no bowels thou!'

'I had rather be a tick in a sheep than such a valiant ignorance.'

'Finch egg!'

Troilus and Cressida

'Many a good hanging prevents a bad marriage.'

'If you be not mad, be gone; if you have reason, be brief.'

'What dish o' poison has she dressed him!'

Twelfth Night

'You, minion, are too saucy.'

'she is peevish, sullen, froward,
 Proud, disobedient, stubborn, lacking duty.'

'Thou friend of an ill fashion!'

The Two Gentlemen of Verona

'Your eye-glass is thicker than a cuckold's horn.'

'I am ... no less honest than you are mad.'

'Female bastard!'

'Stretch-mouth'd rascal!'

The Winter's Tale

The wit of Oscar Wilde

'After a good dinner one can forgive anybody, even one's relations.'

'After playing Chopin, I feel as if I had been weeping over sins that I had never committed, and mourning over tragedies that were not my own.'

'A little sincerity is a dangerous thing, and a great deal of it is absolutely fatal.'

'All charming people, I fancy, are spoiled. It is the secret of their attraction.'

'All women become like their mothers. That is their tragedy. No man does. That's his.'

'A man who moralizes is usually a hypocrite, and a woman who moralizes is invariably plain.'

'Ambition is the last refuge of the failure.'

'America has never quite forgiven Europe for having been discovered somewhat earlier in history than itself.'

'An idea that is not dangerous is unworthy of being called an idea at all.'

'Anybody can sympathize with the sufferings of a friend, but it requires a very fine nature ... to sympathize with a friend's success.'

'Anybody can write a three-volume novel. It merely requires a complete ignorance of both life and literature.'

'As a rule, people who act lead the most commonplace lives.'

'A woman will flirt with anybody in the world as long as other people are looking on.'

'But what is the difference between literature and journalism? Journalism is unreadable and literature is not read. That is all.'

'Children begin by loving their parents; after a time they judge them; rarely, if ever, do they forgive them.'

'Crying is the refuge of plain women, but the ruin of pretty ones.'

'Dammit Sir it's your duty to get married. You can't be always living for pleasure.'

'Details are always vulgar.'

'Duty is what one expects of others, it is not what one does oneself.'

'Education is an admirable thing, but it is well to remember from time to time that nothing that is worth knowing can be taught.'

'Every great man nowadays has his disciples, and it is always Judas who writes the biography.'

'Experience is the name everyone gives to their mistakes.'

'Fathers should be neither seen nor heard. That is the only proper basis for family life.'

'He is a typical Englishman, always dull and usually violent.'

'Hesitation of any kind is a sign of mental decay in the young, of physical weaknesses in the old.'

'I adore simple pleasures. They are the last refuge of the complex.'

'I always like to know everything about my new friends, and nothing about my old ones.'

'I did not sell myself for money. I bought success at a great price.'

'I dislike arguments of any kind. They are always vulgar, and often convincing.'

'I never play cricket. It requires one to adopt such indecent postures.'

'If a women wants to hold a man, she has merely to appeal to what is worst in him.'

'If one cannot enjoy reading a book over and over again, there is no use in reading it at all.'

'If your pistol is as harmless as your pen, this young tyrant will have a long life.'

'I have nothing to declare except my genius.'

'I hope you have not been leading a double life, pretending to be wicked and being really good all the time. That would be hypocrisy.'

'I like men who have a future, and women who have a past.'

'I like to do the talking myself. It saves time and prevents arguments.'

'I was working on the proof of one of my poems all the morning and took out a comma. In the afternoon, I put it back in!'

'Indifference is the revenge the world takes on mediocrities.'

'In examinations the foolish ask questions the wise cannot answer.'

'In matters of grave importance, style, not sincerity, is the vital thing.'

'In the case of very fascinating women, sex is a challenge, not a defence.'

'I quite admit that modern novels have many good points. All I insist on is that, as a class, they are quite unreadable.'

'I sometimes think that God, in creating man, somewhat overestimated his ability.'

'It is always a silly thing to give advice, but to give good advice is absolutely fatal.'

'It is a very dangerous thing to know one's friends.'

'It is the confession, not the priest, that gives us absolution.'

'It is the spectator, and not life, that art really mirrors.'

'It is very difficult sometimes to keep awake,
especially at church.'

'It takes a thoroughly good woman to do a
thoroughly stupid thing.'

'Laughter is not at all a bad beginning for a
friendship, and it is far the best ending for one.'

'Learned conversation is either the affectation of the
ignorant or the profession of the mentally
unemployed.'

'Life is one fool thing after another whereas love is
two fool things after each other.'

'Many a women has a past, but I am told that she has
at least a dozen, and that they all fit.'

'Men become old, but they never become good.'

'Moderation is a fatal thing. Nothing succeeds like
excess.'

'Morality is simply the attitude we adopt towards
people whom we personally dislike.'

'My experience is that as soon people are old enough
to know better, they don't know anything at all.'

'No country produces such badly-written fiction, such tedious, common work in the novel form, such silly, vulgar plays as England.'

'No one cares about distant relatives nowadays. They went out of fashion years ago.'

'One can always be kind to people about whom one cares nothing.'

'One can survive everything nowadays, except death, and live down anything except a good reputation.'

'One should always be in love. That is the reason one should never marry.'

'Really, if the lower orders don't set us a good example, what on earth is the use of them? They seem, as a class, to have absolutely no sense of moral responsibility.'

'Remember that the fool in the eyes of the gods and the fool in the eyes of man are very different.'

'She certainly has a wonderful faculty of remembering people's names, and forgetting their faces.'

'She is like most artists; she is all style without any sincerity.'

'The books that the world calls immoral are books that show the world its own shame.'

'The British public are really not equal to the mental strain of having more than one topic every three months.'

'The conscience of an editor's purely decorative.'

'The English country gentleman galloping after a fox – the unspeakable in full pursuit of the uneatable.'

'The English public, as a mass, takes no interest in a work of art until it is told that the work in question is immoral.'

'The exquisite art of idleness, one of the most important things that any University can teach.'

'The ideal husband? There couldn't be such a thing. The institution is wrong.'

'The man who sees both sides of a question, is a man who sees absolutely nothing at all.'

'The man who would call a spade a spade should be compelled to use one. It is the only thing he is fit for.'

'The only difference between the saint and the sinner is that every saint has a past, and every sinner has a future.'

'The only people to whose opinions I listen now with any respect are people much younger than myself.'

'The only possible form of exercise is to talk, not to walk.'

'The only way a woman can ever reform a man is by boring him so completely that he loses all possible interest in life.'

'There are only two kinds of people who are really fascinating – people who know absolutely everything, and people who know absolutely nothing.'

'There is no sin except stupidity.'

'There is no such thing as a moral or an immoral book. Books are well written, or badly written. That is all.'

'There is only one thing in the world worse than being talked about, and that is not being talked about.'

'The secret of life is never to have an emotion that is unbecoming.'

'The world is a stage, but the play is badly cast.'

'Thinking is the most unhealthy thing in the world and people die of it just as they die of any other disease. Fortunately, in England at any rate, thought is not catching.'

'To get back my youth I would do anything in the world, except take exercise, get up early, or be respectable.'

'To love oneself is the beginning of a lifelong romance.'

'We are all in the gutter, but some of us are looking at the stars.'

'We have really everything in common with America nowadays, except, of course, language.'

'We live in an age that reads too much to be wise, and that thinks too much to be beautiful.'

'We teach people how to remember, we never teach them how to grow.'

'Whenever people agree with me, I always feel I must be wrong.'

'Women are meant to be loved, not to be understood.'

'Women are never disarmed by compliments. Men always are. That is the difference between the two sexes.'

'Woman have a wonderful instinct about things. They can discover everything except the obvious.'

'Work is the refuge of people who have nothing better to do.'

☞ The wisdom of Henry Ward Beecher

'A little library, growing every year, is an honorable part of a man's history. It is a man's duty to have books.'

'A library is not a luxury but one of the necessities of life.'

'All words are pegs to hang ideas on.'

'Books are not made for furniture, but there is nothing else that so beautifully furnishes a house.'

'Books are the true metempsychosis, they are the symbol and presage of immortality.'

'Books are the windows through which the soul looks out.'

'Each book has a secret history of ways and means.'

'Greatness lies not in being strong, but in the right use of strength. '

'Hold yourself responsible for a higher standard than anybody else expects of you. Never excuse yourself. Never pity yourself. Be a hard master to yourself – and be lenient to everybody else.'

'I never knew an early-rising, hard-working, prudent man, careful of his earnings, and strictly honest who complained of bad luck.'

'I never knew how to worship until I knew how to love.'

'Never forget what a man says to you when he is angry.'

'The ability to convert ideas to things is the secret to outward success.'

'The pen is the tongue of the hand; a silent utterer of words for the eye.'

'The soul without imagination is what an observatory would be without a telescope.'

'Where is human nature so weak as in the bookstore?'

☞ **More literary quips and quotes**

'I am returning this otherwise good typing paper to you because someone has printed gibberish all over it and put your name at the top.'

Anonymous response to a novel submitted to a publisher for possible publication

'She is too fond of books, and it has turned her brain.'

Louisa May Alcott

'As a means of shortening your life-span I heartily recommend London.'

'Sex is a momentary itch, love never lets you go.'

Kingsley Amis

'A real book is not one that we read, but one that reads us.'

'The only way to spend New Year's Eve is either quietly with friends or in a brothel. Otherwise when the evening ends and people pair off, someone is bound to be left in tears.'

W.H. Auden

'A woman, especially if she have the misfortune of knowing anything, should conceal it as well as she can.'

'I do not want people to be very agreeable, as it saves me the trouble of liking them a great deal.'

'One half of the world cannot understand the pleasures of the other.'

'A large income is the best recipe for happiness I ever heard of.'

Jane Austen

'If I had been someone not very clever, I would have done an easier job like publishing. That's the easiest job I can think of.'

A.J. Ayer

'For friends ... do but look upon good books: they are true friends that will neither flatter not dissemble.'

'Books will speak plain when counselors blanch.'

'But the images of men's wits and knowledges remain in books, exempted from the wrong of time and capable of perpetual renovation.'

'It is scarce possible at once to admire and excel an author, as water rises no higher than the reservoir it falls from.'

'Libraries are as the shrines where are all the relics of the ancient saints, full of true virtue, and that without delusion or imposture, are preserved and reposed.'

'Some books are to be tasted, others to be swallowed, and some few to be chewed and digested: that is, some books are to be read only in parts, others to be read, but not curiously, and some few to be read wholly, and with diligence and attention.'

Francis Bacon

'The reason why so few good books are written is that so few people who can write know anything.'

Walter Bagehot

'Tradesmen regard an author with a mixed feeling of terror, compassion and curiosity.'

Honoré de Balzac

'The printing press is either the greatest blessing or the greatest curse of modern times, one sometimes forgets which.'

J.M. Barrie

'He was born an Englishman and remained one for years.'

'My grandmother took a bath every year, whether she needed it or not.'

'Other people have a nationality. The Irish and the Jews have a psychosis.'

Brendan Behan

'Always behave as nothing has happened, no matter what has happened.'

Arnold Bennett

'You will find something more in woods than in books. Trees and stones will teach you that which you can never learn from masters.'

St Bernard

'The covers of this book are too far apart.'

Ambrose Bierce

'Do what you will, this world's a fiction and is made up of contradiction.'

William Blake

'But of what use will my book be when it is finished?'

James Boswell

'I am neither a man nor a woman but an author.'

Charlotte Brontë

'Books are men of higher stature, and the only men that speak aloud for future times to hear.'

Elizabeth Barrett Browning

'Friend, howsoever thou camest by this book, I will assure thee thou wert least in my thoughts when I writ it.'

'Some said, "John, print it," others said, "Not so"; Some said, "It might do good," others said, "No".'

John Bunyan

'Writers, especially when they act in a body and with one direction, have great influence on the public mind.'

Edmund Burke

'Some books are lies frae end to end.'

Robert Burns

'There is a kind of physiognomy in the titles of books no less than in the faces of men, by which a skilful observer will as well know what to expect from the one as the other.'

Samuel Butler (1612–1680)

'Cleanliness is almost as bad as godliness.'

'I do not mind lying, but I hate inaccuracy.'

'It is better to have loved and lost than never to have lost at all.'

'Parents are the last people on earth who ought to have children.'

Samuel Butler (1835–1902)

'What men call gallantry, and gods adultery,
Is much more common where the climate's sultry.'

George Gordon, Lord Byron

'All that mankind has done, thought, gained or been: it is lying as in magic preservation in the pages of books.'

'A man ought to inquire and find out what he really and truly has an appetite for, what suits his constitution and condition; and that, doctors tell him, is in general the very thing he ought to have. And so with books.'

'O thou who art able to write a Book, which once in the two centuries or oftener there is a man gifted to do, envy not him whom they name City-builder, and inexpressibly pity him whom they name Conqueror or City-burner!'

'What we become depends on what we read after all of the professors have finished with us. The greatest university of all is a collection of books.'

Thomas Carlyle

'Everything's got a moral, if only you can find it.'

'If you don't know where you are going, any road will get you there.'

Lewis Carroll

'There is no book so bad... but something good may be found in it.'

Miguel de Cervantes Saavedra

'If you liked a book, don't meet the author.'

Raymond Chandler

'A good novel tells us the truth about its hero; but a bad novel tells us the truth about its author.'

'A man does not know what he is saying until he knows what he is not saying.'

'And when it rains on your parade, look up rather than down. Without the rain, there would be no rainbow.'

'A room without books is like a body without a soul.'

'A stiff apology is a second insult. The injured party does not want to be compensated because he has been wronged; he wants to be healed because he has been hurt.'

'Coincidences are spiritual puns.'

'Experience which was once claimed by the aged is now claimed exclusively by the young.'

'I believe in getting into hot water. It keeps you clean.'

'I regard golf as an expensive way of playing marbles.'

'In matters of truth the fact that you don't want to publish something is, nine times out of ten, a proof that you ought to publish it.'

'It is the test of a good religion whether you can joke about it.'

'Literature is a luxury; fiction is a necessity.'

'Music with dinner is an insult both to the cook and the violinist.'

'Once I planned to write a book of poems entirely about the things in my pocket. But I found it would be too long; and the age of the great epics is past.

'People generally quarrel because they cannot argue.'

'Some men never feel small, but these are the few men who are.'

'The mere brute pleasure of reading – the sort of pleasure a cow must have in grazing.'

'The only way to be sure of catching a train is to miss the one before it.'

'The poets have been mysteriously silent on the subject of cheese.'

'There is a great deal of difference between an eager man who wants to read a book and the tired man who wants a book to read.'

'Without education we are in a horrible and deadly danger of taking educated people seriously.'

G.K. Chesterton

'A home without books is a body without soul.'

'For books are more than books, they are the life, the very life and care of ages past, the reason why men worked and died, the essence and quintessence of their lives.'

Marcus Tullius Cicero

'It is saying less than the truth to affirm that an excellent book (and the remark holds almost equally good of a Raphael as of a Milton) is like a well-chosen and well-tended fruit tree. Its fruits are not of one season only. With the due and natural intervals, we may recur to it year after year, and it will supply the same nourishment and the same gratification, if only we ourselves return to it with the same healthful appetite.'

'Let every bookworm, when in any fragrant, scarce old tome, he discovers a sentence, a story, an illustration, that does his heart good, hasten to give it.'

Samuel Taylor Coleridge

'Real poverty is lack of books.'

Sidonie Gabrielle Colette

'He who studies books alone will know how things ought to be, and he who studies men will know how they are.'

'He that will have no books but those that are scarce evinces about as correct a taste in literature as he would do in friendship, who would have no friends but those whom all the rest of the world have sent to Coventry.'

'I have somewhere seen it observed that we should make the same use of a book that the bee does of a flower: she steals sweets from it, but does not injure it.'

'Many books owe their success to the good memories of their authors and the bad memories of their readers.'

'Many books require no thought from those who read them, and for a very simple reason; they made no such demand upon those who wrote them.'

'Next to acquiring good friends, the best acquisition is that of good books.'

'So idle are dull readers, and so industrious are dull authors, that puffed nonsense bids fair to blow unpuffed sense wholly out of the field.'

'That writer does the most who gives his reader the most knowledge, and takes from him the least time.'

'To write what's worth publishing, to find honest people to publish it, and get sensible people to read it, are the three great difficulties in being an author.'

'There are three difficulties in authorship – to write anything worth the publishing, to find honest men to publish it, and to get sensible men to read it.'

Charles Caleb Colton

'An autobiography is an obituary in serial form with the last installment missing.'

'Euphemisms are unpleasant truths wearing diplomatic cologne.'

'Never keep up with the Joneses. Drag them down to your level.'

'Sex is the last refuge of the miserable.'

'The British do not expect happiness. I had the impression, all the time that I lived there, that they do not want to be happy; they want to be right.'

'There are three reasons for becoming a writer: the first is that you need the money; the second that you have something to say that you think the world should know; the third is that you can't think what to do with the long winter evenings.'

'To know all is not to forgive all. It is to despise everybody.'

'You fall out of your mother's womb, you crawl across open country under fire, and drop into your grave.'

Quentin Crisp

'The reading of all good books is like conversation with the noblest men of past centuries who were the authors of them.'

René Descartes

'If you could see my legs when I take my boots off, you'd form some idea of what unrequited affection is.'

'There are books of which the backs and covers are by far the best parts.'

Charles Dickens

'An author who speaks about his own books is almost as bad as a mother who talks about her own children.'

'Of all unfortunate men one of the unhappiest is a middling author endowed with too lively a sensibility for criticism.'

'Thank you for the manuscript; I shall waste no time in reading it.'

'Those authors who appear sometimes to forget they are writers, and remember they are men, will be our favourites.'

'When I want to read a book I write one.'

Benjamin Disraeli

'All authors to their own defects are blind.'

'He who proposed to be an author ought first to be a student.'

John Dryden

'Men love better books which please them than those which instruct. Since their ennui troubles them more than their ignorance, they prefer being amused to being informed.'

Abbé Jean-Antoine Dubois

'Reading, after a certain age, diverts the mind too much from its creative pursuits. Any man who reads too much and uses his own brain too little falls into lazy habits of thinking.'

Albert Einstein

'I've never any pity for conceited people because I think they carry their comfort about with them.'

George Eliot (Mary Anne Evans)

'Every book is a quotation; and every house is a quotation out of all forests and mines and stone quarries; and every man is a quotation from all his ancestors.'

'For no man can write anything who does not think that what he writes is, for the time, the history of the world.'

'If we encounter a man of rare intellect, we should ask him what books he reads.'

'In every man's memory, with the hours when life culminated are usually associated certain books which met his views.'

'In the highest civilization the book is still the highest delight.'

'Never read any book that is not a year old.'

'Some books leave us free and some books make us free.'

'The writer, like a priest, must be exempted from secular labor. His work needs a frolic health; he must be at the top of his condition.'

'We prize books, and they prize them most who are themselves wise.'

'We write from aspiration and antagonism, as well as from experience. We paint those qualities which we do not possess.'

Ralph Waldo Emerson

'Spoon-feeding in the long run teaches us nothing but the shape of the spoon.'

'If I had to choose between betraying my country and betraying my friend, I hope I should have the guts to betray my country.'

E.M. Forster

'For works of the mind really great, there is no old age, no decrepitude. It is inconceivable that a time should come when Homer, Dante, Shakespeare, should not ring in the ears of civilized man.'

William Ewart Gladstone

'Every author, in some degree, portrays himself in his works even be it against his will.'

'If a man writes a book, let him set down only what he knows. I have guesses enough of my own.'

'Properly speaking, we learn only from those books we cannot judge. The author of a book that I am competent to criticize would have to learn from me.'

'The most original modern authors are not so because they advance what is new, but simply because they know how to put what they have to say as if it had never been said before.'

Johann Wolfgang von Goethe

'I armed her against the censures of the world; showed her that books were sweet unreproaching companions to the miserable, and that if they could not bring us to enjoy life, they would at least teach us to endure it.'

'In proportion as society refines, new books must ever become more necessary.'

'In a word, the little mind who loves itself will write and think with the vulgar; but the great mind will be bravely eccentric, and scorn the beaten road, from universal benevolence.'

'Whatever be the motives which induce men to write, whether avarice or fame, the country becomes more wise and happy in which they most serve for instructors.'

Oliver Goldsmith

'I don't think anyone should write their autobiography until after they're dead.'

Sam Goldwyn

'Some folk want their luck buttered.'

Thomas Hardy

'The greatest pleasure in life is that of reading while we are young. I have had as much of this pleasure perhaps as any one.'

'To expect an author to talk as he writes is ridiculous; or even if he did you would find fault with him as a pedant.'

William Hazlitt

'Wherever they burn books, they will also, in the end, burn human beings.'

Heinrich Heine

'Knowledge is the foundation and source of good writing.'

'It shall be consigned to that part of the town where they sell incense, and scents, and pepper, and whatever is wrapped up in worthless paper.'

Horace (Quintus Horatius Flaccus)

'Most human beings have an absolute and infinite capacity for taking things for granted.'

'The news is always bad, even when it sounds good.'

Aldous Huxley

'I like work; it fascinates me. I could sit and look at it for hours.'

Jerome K. Jerome

'A man may write at any time if he set himself doggedly to it.'

'A man will turn over half a library to make one book.'

'A successful author is equally in danger of the diminution of his fame, whether he continues or ceases to write.'

'Books that you may carry to the fire, and hold readily in your hand, are the most useful after all.'

'No man but a blockhead ever wrote, except for money.'

'I never desire to converse with a man who has written more than he has read.'

'No place affords a more striking conviction of the vanity of human hopes than a public library.'

'She is such a sweet lady, only she was so glad to see me go that I have almost a mind to come again, that she may again have the same pleasure.'

'The chief glory of every people arises from its authors.'

'The noblest prospect which a Scotsman ever sees is the high road that leads him to England.'

'The purpose of a writer is to be read, and the criticism which would destroy the power of pleasing must be blown aside.'

'There is nothing more dreadful to an author than neglect; compared with which reproach, hatred, and opposition are names of happiness; yet this worst, this meanest fate, every one who dares to write has reason to fear.'

'There seems to be a strange affectation in authors of appearing to have done everything by chance.'

'What is written without effort is in general read without pleasure.'

'While an author is yet living we estimate his powers by his worst performance, and when he is dead we rate them by his best.'

'Your manuscript is both good and original; but the part that is good is not original, and the part that is original is not good.'

Samuel Johnson

'Books are faithful repositories, which may be awhile neglected or forgotten, but when they are opened again, will again impart their instruction.'

Ben Jonson

'A book must be an ice-axe to break the seas frozen inside our soul.'

Franz Kafka

'Fine writing is, next to fine doing, the top thing in the world.'

John Keats

'A woman is only a woman, but a good cigar is a smoke.'

'A woman's guess is much more accurate than a man's certainty.'

'An ounce of mother is worth a pound of clergy.'

'That the female of the species is more deadly than the male.'

'God could not be everywhere, and therefore he made mothers.'

'He travels the fastest who travels alone.'

'I always prefer to believe the best of everybody; it saves so much trouble.'

'It's clever, but is it Art?'

'Never look backwards or you'll fall down the stairs.'

'Words are, of course, the most powerful drug used by mankind.'

Rudyard Kipling

'We ought to reverence books, to look at them as useful and mighty things. If they are good and true, whether they are about religion, politics, farming, trade, law or medicine, they are the message of Christ, the maker of all things, the teacher of all truth.'

Charles Kingsley

'I love to lose myself in other men's minds. When I am not walking, I am reading; I cannot sit and think. Books think for me.'

Charles Lamb

'A book is a friend whose face is constantly changing. If you read it when you are recovering from an illness, and return to it years after, it is changed surely, with the change in yourself.'

Andrew Lang

'I don't know much about creative writing programs. But they're not telling the truth if they don't teach, one, that writing is hard work, and, two, that you have to give up a great deal of life, your personal life, to be a writer.'

'Literature is analysis after the event.'

Doris Lessing

'Everyone says that forgiveness is a lovely idea, until
they have something to forgive.'

C.S. Lewis

'Books serve to show a man that those original
thoughts of his aren't very new after all.'

Abraham Lincoln

'If you once understand an author's character, the
comprehension of his writings becomes easy.'

'Perhaps the greatest lesson which the lives of
literary men teach us is told in a single world: Wait!'

'The love of learning, the sequestered nooks,
And all the sweet serenity of books.'

Henry Wadsworth Longfellow

'Every great book is an action, and every great action
is a book.'

Martin Luther

'He felt about books as doctors feel about medicines,
or managers about plays – cynical, but hopeful.'

Rose Macaulay

'I am Envy. I cannot read and therefore wish all
books burned.'

Christopher Marlowe

'From the moment I picked your book up until I laid it down I was convulsed with laughter. Some day I intend reading it.'

'I find television very educating. Every time someone turns on the set I go into the other room and read a book.'

Groucho Marx

'An author spends months writing a book, and maybe puts his heart's blood into it, and then it lies about unread til the reader has nothing else in the world to do.'

'Only a mediocre author is always at his best.'

'There are three rules for writing a novel. Unfortunately, no one knows what they are.'

'Tolerance is only another word for indifference.'

'To write simply is as difficult as to be good.'

'You have a magnificent chance, with all the advantages of wealth and position. Don't throw it away by any exhibition of talent.'

W. Somerset Maugham

'Bores can be divided into two classes; those who have their own particular subject, and those who do not need a subject.'

'What I say is this, if a fellow really likes potatoes, he must be a pretty decent sort of fellow.'

A.A. Milne

'A good book is the precious life-blood of a master spirit imbalmed and treasured up on purpose to a life beyond life.'

'Books are not absolutely dead things, but do contain a potency of life in them to be as active as that soul was whose progeny they are; nay, they do preserve as in a vial the purest efficacy and extraction of that living intellect that bred them.'

'Deep versed in books and shallow in himself.'

'He who destroys a good book, kills reason itself.'

'Many a man lives a burden upon the earth; but a good book is the precious life-blood of a master spirit, embalmed and treasured up on purpose for a life beyond life.'

John Milton

'When I am attacked by gloomy thoughts, nothing helps me so much as running to my books. They quickly absorb me and banish the clouds from my mind.'

Michel de Montaigne

'It is my ambition to say in ten sentences what others say in a whole book.

Friedrich Nietzsche

'You can't be a rationalist in an irrational world. It isn't rational.'

Joe Orton

'A family with the wrong members in control; that, perhaps, is as near as one can come to describing England in a phrase.'

'There is only one way to make money at writing and that is to marry a publisher's daughter.'

George Orwell (Eric Blair)

'I believe that a man may write himself out of reputation when nobody else can do it.'

Thomas Paine

'I don't care what is written about me, as long as it isn't true.'

'This is not a novel to be tossed aside lightly. It should be thrown with great force.'

Dorothy Parker

'The last thing that we discover in writing a book is to know what to put at the beginning.'

Blaise Pascal

'We saw *Midsummer's Night's Dream*, which I had never seen before, nor shall ever see again, for it is the most insipid, ridiculous play that ever I saw in my life.'

Samuel Pepys

'Authors, like coins, grow dear as they grow old;
It is the rust we value, not the gold.'

'To buy books only because they were published by an eminent printer is much as if a man should buy clothes that did not fit him, only because made by some famous tailor.'

'True ease in writing comes from art, not chance,
As those move easiest who have learn'd to dance.'

Alexander Pope

'Everything must be put back in its proper disorder.'

Barbara Pym

'Books may be burned and cities sacked, but truth, like the yearning for freedom, lives in the hearts of humble men and women.'

Franklin Delano Roosevelt

'All books are divisible into two classes, the books of the hour, and the books of all time.'

'Great nations write their autobiographies in three manuscripts – the book of their deeds, the book of their words and the book of their art.'

'No human being, however great, or powerful, was ever so free as a fish.'

'Nothing can be beautiful which is not true.'

'Tell me what you like and I'll tell you what you are.'

'When a man is wrapped up in himself, he makes a pretty small package.'

'Whereas it has long been known and declared that the poor have no right to the property of the rich, I wish it also to be known and declared that the rich have no right to the property of the poor.'

John Ruskin

'If one hides one's talents under a bushel, one must be careful to point out to everyone the exact bushel under which it is hidden.'

'A little misery wouldn't matter very much with her; it would go so well with the way she does her hair.'

Saki (Hector Hugh Munro)

'Any book which is at all important should be re-read immediately.'

Arthur Schopenhauer

'A multitude of books distracts the mind.'

Socrates

'An index is a great leveller.'

'Englishmen will never be slaves; they are free to do whatever the Government and public opinion allow them to do.'

'If you eliminate smoking and gambling, you will be amazed to find that almost all an Englishman's pleasures can be, and mostly are, shared by his dog.'

'It is impossible for an Englishman to open his mouth without making some other Englishman hate or despise him.'

'Patriotism is your conviction that this country is superior to all other countries because you were born in it.'

'Syllables govern the world.'

'The secret of being miserable is to have leisure to bother about whether you are happy or not.'

'What really flatters a man is that you think him worth flattering.'

George Bernard Shaw

'No furniture is so charming as books.'

Sydney Smith

'Give me a room whose every nook is dedicated to a book.'

Robert Southey

'Every book is, in an intimate sense, a circular-letter to the friends of him who writes it.'

Robert Louis Stevenson

'I have lost all sense of home, having moved about so much. It means to me now – only that place where the books are kept.'

John Steinbeck

'Would a writer know how to behave himself with relation to posterity, let him consider in old books what he finds that he is glad to know, and what omissions he most laments.'

'Books, the children of the brain.'

Jonathan Swift

'If the secret history of books could be written, and the author's private thoughts and meanings noted down alongside of his story, how many insipid volumes would become interesting, and dull tales excite the reader.'

'The two most engaging powers of an author are to make new things familiar, familiar things new.'

William Makepeace Thackeray

'Oh, isn't life a terrible thing, thank God?'

Dylan Thomas

'At least let us have healthy books.'

'Books are the treasured wealth of the world and the fit inheritance of generations and nations.'

'Books can only reveal us to ourselves, and as often as they do us this service we lay them aside.'

'It is not all books that are as dull as their readers.'

'Nothing goes by luck in composition. It allows of no tricks. The best you can write will be the best you are. Every sentence is the result of a long probation. The author's character is read from title-page to end.'

'Read the best books first, or you may not have a chance to read them at all.'

'The book exists for us, perchance, which will explain our miracles and reveal new ones.'

'The books that help you most are those which make you think that most. The hardest way of learning is that of easy reading; but a great book that comes from a great thinker is a ship of thought, deep freighted with truth and beauty.'

Henry David Thoreau

'No man thinks there is much ado about nothing when the ado is about himself.'

Anthony Trollope

'Nothing sickens me more than the closed door of a library.'

Barbara Tuchman

'Age is an issue of mind over matter. If you don't mind, it doesn't matter.'

'A natural death is where you die by yourself without the aid of a doctor.'

'Be careful about reading health books. You may die of a misprint.'

'Children have become so expensive that only the poor can afford them.'

'Great books are weighed and measured by their style and matter and not by the trimmings and shadings of their grammar.'

'Just the omission of Jane Austen's books alone would make a fairly good library out of a library that hadn't a book in it.'

'Substitute "damn" every time you're inclined to write "very"; your editor will delete it and the writing will be just as it should be.'

Mark Twain

'Anything too stupid to be said is sung.'

'A small number of choice books are sufficient.'

'Common sense is not so common.'

'Doubt is a not a pleasant condition, but certainty is absurd.'

'Every man is guilty of all the good he did not do.'

'He must be very ignorant for he answers every question he is asked.'

'In every author let us distinguish the man from his works.'

'It is with books as with men: a very small number play a great part; the rest are confounded with the multitude.'

'Marriage is the only adventure open to the cowardly.'

'The secret of being boring is to say everything.'

'To succeed in the world it is not enough to be stupid, you must also be well-mannered.'

Voltaire (François-Marie Arouet)

'Anyone could write a novel given six weeks, pen, paper and no telephone or wife.'

'Manners are especially the need of the plain. The pretty can get away with anything.'

'My father spent the last twenty years of his life writing letters. If someone thanked him for a wedding present, he thanked them for thanking him and there was no end to the exchange but death.'

Evelyn Waugh

'In England, we have come to rely upon a comfortable time-lag of fifty years or a century intervening between the perception that something ought to be done and a serious attempt to do it.'

H.G. Wells

'It is queer how it is always one's virtues and not one's vices that precipitate one into disaster.'

Rebecca West

'The dirtiest book of all is the expurgated one.'

Walt Whitman

'I would never read a book if it were possible for me to talk half an hour with the man who wrote it.'

Thomas Woodrow Wilson

'I would venture to guess that Anon, who wrote so many poems without signing them, was often a woman.'

'Second-hand books are wild books, homeless books; they have come together in vast flocks of variegated feather, and have a charm which the domesticated volumes of the library lack.'

'Those comfortably padded lunatic asylums which are known, euphemistically, as the stately homes of England.'

Virginia Woolf

'This dull product of a scoffer's pen.'

William Wordsworth

'I think it better that in times like these a poet's mouth be silent, for in truth we have no gift to set a statesman right.'

'There are no strangers here; only friends you haven't yet met.'

W.B. Yeats